# BATTLE
# TACTICS

BASIC INSTRUCTIONS FOR SPIRITUAL WARFARE

VINCENT E. GOARD

Printed in the United States of America

THIS BOOK IS NOT INTENDED TO BE A HISTORY TEXT. While every effort has been made to check the accuracy of dates, locations, and historical information, no claims are made as to the accuracy of such information.

For bulk book orders, author appearance inquiries, and interviews, contact the author via the guestbook at www.VincentGoard.com or Call business office 415-787-3784.

Cover Art is an original acrylic 24"x 36" canvas piece called 'Duality' by artist, Mary Elise. Used with permission, all rights reserved by Mary Elise Art.

ISBN: 9781688725027

# DEDICATION

*I dedicate this work to my Commander and King Jesus to whom I am eternally grateful to serve as ambassador of and son in this glorious Gospel of His Kingdom.*

*To my wife, Toemeika, because you are the Love of God incarnate. In retrospect I think the Lord was trying to use you to teach me these concepts from the very beginning of our marriage, I'm a slow study but I'm learning. Thank you for everything Babygirl.*

*To my children, Seth, Zoie, & Carlie who serve as daily reminders of the favor of God, I am so blessed to have you.*

*To my Family, thank you for the love, support, encouragement, and prayers.*

*To my Catalyst Family for laboring and sharing the Gospel with me to the world in Love, Instruction, and Demonstration. ;)*

*To Mama Julia & Auntie Al for helping me capture and polish this work.*

*Finally, to every Pastor, Leader, and person who has ever dealt with suicidal depression and your still here. You have too much work to do, he is trying to get you to hurt yourself because he can't.*

# FOREWORD

Battle Tactics is a book that every believer should read. Pastor Vincent Goard has superbly supplied the plan every believer needs in order to win the spiritual battle in which they are currently engaged. The Bible states that before a king makes war, he must first consider what it will take for him to win the war. Battle Tactics gives a believer an opportunity to gain some insight about the enemy they are fighting and provides a strategy for victory. By presenting the who, what, when, where, why and how of the strategic battle plan, Pastor Goard has provided valuable information for believers, at every spiritual level, to be able to successfully engage the enemy. No matter if you have been recently saved or have been walking with the Lord for decades, Battle Tactics will help you in your spiritual walk. I believe as you read Battle Tactics, it will help you to focus your energies, so as you fight your spiritual battle, you will be victorious!

Curt W. Buckmire, Senior Pastor

Spirit and Truth International Worship Center, Loganville, GA.

# TABLE OF CONTENTS

# INTRODUCTION

This book is based on a message series the Lord gave me near the end of a dark time in my life this past year. Unfortunately, it is not the product of some amazing victory as you may assume with a title like "Battle Tactics", as if I was some coach with a legendary winning streak giving out copies of his coveted playbook. No, this is the result of failure... and lots of it. Failure in my marriage, my parenting, my mission, and in my personal and corporate service in ministry. The depression and disappointment as a result were so tangible that for a while, I was contemplating self-harm. I realized that suicide would only leave my family in a worse condition, unprotected from my foolishness and me in an impossible situation, committing a sin to which I would later not have the breath to repent from. It was almost as if the Lord, like a lifeguard at the beach, waited until I was done struggling internally to rescue me from myself. He showed me that I was never going to be able to win the way I was working.

My knowledge of how to be a man of God, a husband, and father, would only be successful if I better understood my God and my opposition better. Like a corner coach in a boxing match that tells His fighter how to recover based on what He sees the combatant doing; God was showing me the way the enemy was attacking because He can see from all angles. My blind spots became my confidence and stagnation which were causing me to lose, taking on too much damage.

Growing up, we were told that "Experience is the best teacher", but it has become painfully clear to me that is not the truth. Obedience is the best teacher; Experience is the substitute teacher that shows up to when your Obedience is sick. The Lord shared with me things that were happening that I kept failing in because of pride and ignorance, but no longer! The way we win now is by being obedient to His instructions and information.

Prayerfully friend, the content of this book will help you grow in grace as we talk about proper training and preparing your spirit man for this warfare and then, learn:

➤ WHO is your enemy?
➤ WHAT he wants to steal?
➤ WHEN he will attack?
➤ WHERE he will attack?
➤ WHY the enemy hates you?
➤ HOW he will do it?

⚠ Caution! If you continue past this point you won't be able to live in ignorance and your status on the enemy's most wanted list will be upgraded!

You still here? Good! I hoped you would not let fear stop you. Well, it seems we have a brave one here! ......Ok,...... let us begin. Prepare yourself for revelation and fellowship with our King that will cause us to live in victory despite our opposition. If God be for us, who can be against us!

Momentum only,
Vince

# 1: The Beginning

Friend, I want to break down the Who, What, When, Where, Why, and the How of our oppositions battle tactics. During the course of these pages and chapters, we will address how we should operate concerning Kingdom Warfare, but I am going to make this statement often: we are in the middle of a war all the time. There are two kingdoms that are actively at war. One already has the victory. The other one is trying to usurp authority. Now, here's how this works. When we choose whose side, we're on, it makes a lot of difference on how we experience this life. Making the wrong choice will cause us to fight the wrong fight. Faulting the issues, we wrestle with and the things we go through to an individual or a situation. It's not that at all. It's much bigger than that.

As a matter of fact, it's bigger than me and you combined. It is not about us but rather, is totally on an infinite level. We just happen to be finite chess pieces on the board of life that get commissioned as part of this battle. Here's the thing though. If we allow the Lord to be the King of our life, we get the opportunity to win.

Notice that I used the words choose and allow, our God is a gentleman and He is not going to force you to choose Him. As much as He loves you and wants you to, the situations in our lives are often part of a greater plan where He is proving how much He believes in us. That like Job, He allows matters and situations for us to identify what He already knows is in us. Before we go too far, let's establish the sides by the one thing that defines it, the Gospel of the Kingdom of God.

## Disappointment in Missions

In March 2012, my best friend, Michael Southwell, coordinated my first international missions' trip to the eastern Caribbean island of St. Lucia. I was one of four pastors in a group of twenty total people. He arranged for me to be a part of the smaller set-up team, so we touched down a few days earlier to help him prepare for the larger portion of the team to show up. The northern half of the island is where the cruise ships would port so it was very commercial to accommodate the tourists. We were stationed on the south side by the international airport. It was moving to be on the local's side of the island as it showed signs it was still recovering from the damage almost sixteen months prior by Hurricane Tomas.

Now, Michael is a true prophet and has a gift of connecting people and resources in the body of Christ. (Ask me one day to share the story about how the Lord used him to confirm my bride). Anyone he had vetted for this trip I felt compelled to intentionally honor and respect, but this group and our host were easy to love. Once the remaining portion of the team showed up the host pastor had arranged for us to split up to do door to door witnessing in the daytime. Then in the evening open-air tent services that they called Crusades in four different locations that we were assigned to each night.

Now our host pastor was a prominent Bishop on the island and his church's lower floor is where we setup base camp. Although we were sleeping in sleeping bags on the floor, I was excited because I thought living without my regular creature comforts meant that I was suffering for the Kingdom. The team that was from Atlanta, commented that we were just "taking the Gospel on vacation" because of how beautiful the setting was and that this was not a true mission's trip. Trying not to feel insulted at their comments, I continued through. It would take some years, and a few additional international missions' destinations later for me to realize that they were right.

It wasn't until about our second day with the whole team onsite that I noticed that each night when we would return to base to share what happened at our separate locations the group from Atlanta had these amazing stories of miracles. There was a growth that disappeared off a man's back, and a woman with a blind eye whose sight was restored, and I was bothered. The day before they got there, I had the privilege of praying with a family that had 1 of a pair of twin babies that was sick.

The baby's bowel had ruptured internally, her belly was distended, and her eyes were jaundice. The local soccer stadium was retrofitted to serve as a hospital as the new one was not finished from the storm. The doctors gave her a 40% chance of survival with a surgery and the family had requested the church to come before they decided. As we made our hospital visit, I noticed that there was no monitoring equipment, only an oxygen tank, a piece of plywood board that was separating this room into smaller stations, and a small container of Vaseline brand petroleum jelly by the bed.

When I was asked to pray, I didn't hesitate. In my excitement, I dipped my finger in the Vaseline to substitute for anointing oil, touched the baby's head and prayed every scripture concerning healing that I knew over that baby. Surely, God was going to show up and heal this baby because this was my first missions' trip! I thought to myself, "I'm out here Lord, I left my church and family for ten days", so I just knew this baby is going to be healed!

When I was finished praying, I encouraged the mom to speak over the baby that night and I asked the host if we could follow up with them later in the trip to get the testimony. It was the day before the rest of the team showed up, so I was excited to see God move early in the trip, only the baby died that night.

The next morning the host asked if we wanted to go with them to see the family and I conveniently gave an excuse that we were working on the setup for the rest of the team. Personally, my pride was wounded, and I was embarrassed. The team was arriving, and Crusades were about to begin, and I angrily asked God "why? I know you could have done it, why did you let that happen?". Just as clearly, He spoke back to me "Son, you never asked what My will was concerning the situation. You tried to force My hand so you could take the glory". I wept quietly, because it was hard to hear and even harder to believe.

It was a challenge to get my head back focused as we sorted the team and completed our first nights of Crusade. So, by the time I had gotten out of my mental fog I realized that the stories were coming from the team that was from and how young they were. Atlanta All fresh twenty somethings who were radically turned on to Jesus I got quiet and listened. Their pastor was a tanned California surfer dude who was clearly their senior but had more energy than all of them put together. He was my roommate, and his name was Dan. That night nothing but preaching and singing happened at my location so I didn't contribute much.

As if by divine design, the team was going to bed so we could prepare for our community service project in the morning and Michael called me over to speak with

Dan. "Show him what you just showed me!" Michael says and then walks away. What Dan showed me that night changed my walk with God forever. It was to be the reason I had to fly six hours away from my family and comfort zone to sit with someone who, back home, was literally six exits down the highway from me. It was to hear what I'm about to share with you. He has an amazing, much more polished presentation but here is my version of it.

## Defining the Gospel

If I was to ask you what is the Gospel, what would you say? The Good News... It's about Jesus and how much He loves us.... About Him dying on the cross for our sins.... How He rose again on the third day with all power...

Absolutely, that would be the common answer...and there is nothing wrong with that. It's the message preached over pulpits and on street corners all the time. ...all of those facts are correct, only that's not the whole answer. Before you start to close this book and look for a match to burn it, let's go to Luke 9:1-6. It states:

*vs[1] Then he called his twelve disciples together, and <u>gave them power and authority over all devils, and to cure diseases.</u>*

*vs<sup>2</sup> And <u>he sent them to preach the kingdom of God</u>, and to heal the sick.*

*vs<sup>3</sup> And he said unto them, Take nothing for your journey, neither staves, nor scrip, neither bread, neither money; neither have two coats apiece.*

*vs<sup>4</sup> And whatsoever house ye enter into, there abide, and thence depart.*

*vs<sup>5</sup> And whosoever will not receive you, when you go out of that city, shake off the very dust from your feet for a testimony against them.*

*vs<sup>6</sup> <u>And they departed, and went through the towns, preaching the gospel,</u> and healing every where.*

Now, as we go through scripture, I'm going to underline the areas of emphasis so that they stand out prominently for the rest of this book. Here we see Jesus preparing to dispatch the disciples and in the first verse, He assembles them and then empowers them. He gives them power over all devils and to cure diseases. Verse 2 specifically states that He sent them to preach the ... say it with me, "Kingdom of God". Vs 3-5 is Jesus describing what to anticipate on their outreach, but it is in vs 6 that we see something different. As if to document their launching, it states they left, going from town to town "preaching the Gospel". Look again vs 2 reads "preach the Kingdom of God" and vs 6 replaces it with "the Gospel".

11

Now, hold your finger against your temple and let's think, are they preaching about the Death, Burial, and Resurrection of Christ? That doesn't happen for at least another twelve chapters in the book of Luke.

Now go to Luke 18:31-34, by now we have had some significant miracles performed in Jesus ministry. The disciples have had the opportunity to go out a few times preaching, and miracles have happened in their outreaches. Here Jesus is about to tell them something He has never told them before, watch their reaction.

*vs³¹ Then he took unto him the twelve, and said unto them, <u>Behold, we go up to Jerusalem,</u> <u>and all things that</u> <u>are written by the prophets concerning the Son of man</u> <u>shall be accomplished.</u>*

*vs³² For <u>he shall be delivered unto the Gentiles,</u> and shall be mocked, and spitefully entreated, and spitted on:*

*vs³³ And <u>they shall scourge him, and put him to death:</u> <u>and the third day he shall rise again.</u>*

*vs³⁴ <u>And they understood none of these things</u>: and this saying was hid from them, neither knew they the things which were spoken.*

Pay attention, Jesus is just NOW telling His disciples, after 3 years of preaching and fellowshipping with Him that He is going to be put to death and rise on the third day. The most powerful part is vs 34 reads in three different ways that, they did not understand what Jesus was speaking of, they were totally oblivious.

How is the good news about a cross when they are just now hearing about it? And, what have they been preaching for the past three years?

## The King and His Kingdom

In Matthew 4, after being tempted in the wilderness the first thing Jesus says is Repent for the Kingdom of Heaven is at hand. Later in chapter 6:33 it states

*vs<sup>33</sup> But <u>seek ye first the kingdom of God, and his righteousness</u>; and all these things shall be added unto you.*

Noticing a pattern? The word Kingdom is a compound word. The "King" which represents one who rules in complete authority. The "dom" is short for dominion, which is the area or place that is subject to the ruler along with His culture and ways. A culture consists of the laws, language, customs, currency, and climate of a people.

In essence He challenges us to repent for The Ruler and His culture and ways are present. This eludes to the idea that a fake or substitute ruler is in position. The Righteousness in vs 33 requires us to seek this King and His culture and to submit to His culture at His standard of living. This Gospel or Good News is that there is a King who has come to rescue us from a kingdom rule contrary to God and His glory. Mark 1:14-15 states it a little more precisely:

*vs^14 Now after that John was put in prison, <u>Jesus came into Galilee, preaching the gospel of the kingdom of God,</u>*

*vs^15 And saying, The time is fulfilled, and <u>the kingdom of God is at hand: repent ye, and believe the gospel</u>.*

The purpose of Jesus ministry was to establish His Kingdom here. If we read the bible for ourselves looking for a savior, well then it makes the Gospel about saving us. If we read this bible as a chronicle of a King who has come to reclaim what rightfully always belonged to Him, we discover a mystery that has been hidden in plain sight.

See, when all we see Him as is a savior, then we are never challenged to seek His Person as to who He is. Then we only want His Power, as if He is a get-out-of-Hell-free-card. If we don't listen to His message to repent as He warns us that something is out of place, then we end up taking His Place at the throne, fulfilling our own will and way establishing our own culture or standard of righteousness.

He absolutely was a Messiah. He was a King. That's why Pilate succumbed to the pressure of the Pharisees. Driving him to crucify Christ for committing treason against Cesar for declaring His Kingdom for 3 years. (John 18:28-37) He is even questioned and responds that, "Yes, I am a King, but if my Kingdom was of this realm my people wouldn't let you touch me". Yet, ironically the ones who committed the treason was us.

The Gospel is the Kingdom of God, and the Good News is that mankind can be redeemed from its bad state. We are participating in a war and defaultly we've been born on the wrong side of this Kingdom. Sin has separated us and placed us in a treasonous position that requires judgement. Here is why His blood was shed, the punishment for treason requires death.

## The 3 Day Work vs 3 Year Work

It seemed as if time slowed as Dan walked me through the scriptures that were always there in my Bible, but for whatever reason never read so loudly and so clear. The Lord had been showing me the pieces of a puzzle, but Dan knew what the picture was supposed to be. He began to frame up a Gospel that I, as a pastor, was now even more embarrassed that I had not found. Seeing as at this point, I had been a senior pastor for twelve years I was thinking about all the revivals, sermons, and youth events I had preached at over the many years of my ministry thinking I have misled His people.

Was this why the young people were on fire? Lord why didn't you show me this earlier? Weren't you concerned about all those people I was in front of? He softly said, "It's not about you. It was never about you, but I am showing you now". I realized that I had fallen in love with the work of the Lord and forgotten the Lord of the work... Now, face down, I was not much more than a snotty wet spot on a six-foot folding table repenting. Once again it was a hard truth, that I had been preaching a partial gospel. One that now I understand helped me lose sight of the Lord I loved and audibly heard as a boy in my bedroom growing up. It was one that I now call the 3-day Gospel.

It is the Gospel you described in the beginning of this chapter. The one where He loved me so much that He died for me so I could have life and then rose again to give me power over death, Hell, and the grave. Sound familiar? Sound selfish?

For years I had been preaching about a 3-day work and totally neglected these chapters that clearly describe the 3-year message of Gospel of the Kingdom of God. The one that came with signs and wonders, the one that required me to not be the narrative at all but submit to this King and His Kingdom which was, and is, and is to come.

God showed me this image as I meditated on the words I was given.

Imagine building a house, no one starts with the door. They start with a good foundation, then frame, sheetrock, insulation, plumbing, electrical, HVAC, siding, and so on. One of the last things that gets installed is the door.

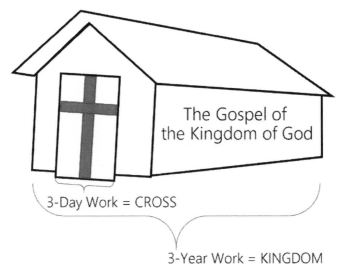

3-Day Work = CROSS

3-Year Work = KINGDOM

Created by V.Goard ©

Looking at this diagram, the house represents the Kingdom of God. The message Jesus and the disciples preached that healed the sick and raised the dead. The fulfilment of prophecy from the Old Testament being lived in the flesh by the Son of God. The cross on the door, it is our entry point into the Kingdom as Jesus clearly says in John 14:6, "I am the way, the truth, and the life: no man cometh unto the Father, but by me". The 3-day work that we preach is the finishing touch to the 3-year message of the Kingdom of God.

Once we enter in, then there is so much more to master and mature in that we must progress to get to know the Lord and King better.

That night, I repented of doing a good work and was grateful He extended me mercy because my heart was ready for the full Gospel. I gained a brother in Dan as I continue in the Gospel even to this day. Now, don't get me wrong, I am not implying that I am a wonderful example of our King's Words. The Lord is still walking me through the areas that need work in my life, one subject, one issue, and one stronghold at a time.

The problem was I was missing the interference and ploys of the enemy. I kept falling for them while trying so hard to measure up to a level of expectation for God that I had created in my mind and was not allowing Him to settle my heart so I could just be His, which is why you are now holding this book.

Kind of like the person who is trying so hard to impress that they only make an even worse mess of things. Friend I pray this helps you as I am just beginning to own this now: The King is already impressed with you!

That's why He wants you to surrender to Him. This is a call to recruitment, because if you have not asked Jesus to be your King but only your Savior, you have not submitted totally. The power of what we will go over in the next chapters will be wasted if we don't address this first. You may have given your life to the Lord and gotten baptized, you may have grown up in church and feel as if you have a defined relationship, you may even be leading a powerful ministry and discipling others... Friend, I was all of those things and yet the Lord had mercy on me because there was a small portion that I was ignorant to and when it was shared with me ...the same way I am sharing it to you now... it was because the Lord loved me but required me to raise my level of commitment and grow in my surrender.

To get the benefit of being on the right side of this war, would you mind praying this prayer with me?

'Lord Jesus, I repent of The Sin, that put me in a position of treason against Your rule in my life. Be my King, and I will be careful to serve as an ambassador and be accepted as a child. Being content to be loved, and not earn it, and return Your love by obedience, amen.'

Friend, right now all of Heaven is rejoicing over you and your confession. If you prayed that prayer with sincerity of heart, you are now fully inducted into the Kingdom of God. This was the most dynamic confession that sets you aligned with the culture of our King. I am not going to lie to you and tell you your life is going to be all easy from now on, only that you have access to reinforcements in times of turmoil.

What this has also done is made you an enemy of the kingdom of darkness but don't worry, you're in good hands now. Make sure to find a Bible teaching ministry that has a fellowship of believers that are pressing to grow in proficiency of the Word as well as in action of it. Ask your pastor to be baptized and to receive the infilling of the Holy Spirit. Participate in the church, study the word of God, pray every day, and grow in maturity. Most of all share the gospel you have, don't wait till you know it all...because you never will. Share what you have, and watch lives change for His glory.

# 2: Sharing the King of Kings

## Preach Who He is, .....not what He does

My wife and I will celebrate 22 years of marriage this year. Even though I have known her for 37 years, I learn something new about her all the time. I'd like to think that I have an Associate's Degree in Toemeika, and I have soooo much to still learn. When we first got married, she was just a cute face, a soprano voice, and long hair, with spaghetti legs and meatball knees. During our first years, I learned she was a big sports fan, to the point she could tell you who someone got traded to and went pro. She is an excellent cook, and what kind of husband would I be if I wasn't her test subject. She is sort-of-a-shade-tree mechanic, knowing just enough to be able to walk into AutoZone and call out parts by the number (she used to work there). We've had many great moments and growing pains over the years but she is my wife.

When we speak of Jesus, we talk about His saving power. That He is a healer and deliverer. That He is a provider and our peace. The problem with that is if that is all we say about Him we are giving a partial description of an overwhelming God. We introduce people to what He can do, but not to who He is. When Jesus stands before Pilate (John 18:26-40) being asked if He was King of the Jews, His reply was that He was a King but not of this realm. When the disciples shared the Gospel according to Luke 6, they preached the Kingdom of God. Not the Cross, but the Crown. Now don't get me wrong, the Cross is necessary, but it is only a benefit to those who submit to the Crown. The reason I began this section about my wife is that she can do many things, however, those are only benefits of what she does for me. It does not define who she is. She is my wife, not my chef, my sports resource, mechanic, or my trophy.

Again, we have to be sure to not create interest in what He does because then it opens the door for people to want that instead of just Him. He is a KING, that saves. Let's be intentional about introducing Him that way. That way when our enemy presents himself people will not be drawn away and offended because they expected something from God that satan lied about. Let's be clear on who we serve and how we serve Him so we can clearly see the plans and tactics of the enemy.

# YOUR ENEMY: A Tactical Spiritual Dossier

Now from here forward, we are going to expose the enemy and how he operates. I encourage you to get a pen and write in the margins, take notes, and get your bible to read and reference all the scriptures as we go forward. No turning back now... Defining our Enemy.

# 3. The WHO

## Look Harder, Follow the Strings
A lesson in discernment

Imagine an animal that was poorly taken care of, its owner didn't feed it well, abused it, and trained it to attack anyone. Do you fault the pet for its actions? Of course not. Do they suffer sometimes for the result of their actions? Yes. Weirdly enough, that same pet will defend the abusive owner just because it doesn't know any better and thinks that this is the only way to cope until in some cases, they can no longer take it.

Now, visualize your favorite TV puppet, you know, like Cookie Monster, Big Bird, or Elmo. When you watch them on screen, they seem alive as the puppeteer manipulates the subject, adding dialogue and gestures to bring them to life, but do you believe what you see to be true? Although the puppeteer works hard to create the image of them being independent, and the studio set and camera angles hide the evidence, they are being moved by something else.

Am I calling the people who are in our lives puppets or animals? No, I am saying that no matter how good or holy they are, people can become tools being used in that moment to distract us from what is really happening. It is in these moments that we have to first take people at face value, remembering that we were all born in sin and shaped in iniquity (Psalms 51:1; Romans 5:12). It is in our DNA, even Paul declares his struggle referencing that when he would want to do good, evil is always present (Romans 7:21).

When people justify their sins by saying they were "born that way", I don't fight their argument, because it is "that" reason Jesus tells us we must be born again! Realize that they are being the best them they can be at that moment and even though you can see better in them or hope for their maturity and growth... you got what ya' got today. Don't take it personal, then we can look past what we see in front of us.

There are coping mechanisms that they have learned to use to justify their lives that keep them in a place that makes them easy fodder for our true enemy to manipulate and exaggerate. In other cases, people have created ways of living that can be used by our true enemy to inflict pain in our lives. It is not totally their fault. Hurt people often hurt other people, and all of us must give an account to God of the actions taken in our flesh (Romans 14:12). It is being able to separate the offence from the offenders. Much like Jesus, we must learn to forgive the individual and so we can address the real enemy (Luke 23:34).

Let's go to the scripture to three examples and "follow the strings" to see what or who is truly motivating the actions documented. In the first two of these examples God speaks to His prophet to address a king who is in power. As we read, we will see in both passages that God speaks to the person in position, then changes the message and addresses the true enemy, satan.

In Ezekiel 28, the royal family of Tyre are the persons in position who is operating against God's intent. God sends Ezekiel to confront the prince for his actions in vs 1 - 5. Vs 2 captures the words that the prince declares putting himself on this shortlist of correction from God. Listen to his confession paying close attention to the portion underlined:

"*Because thine heart is lifted up, and thou hast said, I am a God, I sit in the seat of God, in the midst of the seas; yet thou art a man, and not God, though thou set thine heart as the heart of God*".

The prince is committing treason against The Highest Throne, God's, and his heart is the issue (Jeremiah 17:9). The pride that has filled his heart and convinced him that he is as great as God was a combination of his own desire and the culture that was modeled in front of him by his father the king of Tyre. Vs 6 - 10 describe the punishment for his actions.

Its vs 11 where things get very peculiar, God tells the prophet in vs 12 to take up "a lamentation upon the king of Tyre" or in other words literally "cry" for him. Almost like the parent who after correcting their child has to go away to collect themselves because it hurt them to have to punish the child. Then Ezekiel was instructed to deliver a message to the king, only this time pay attention to the words in the message as you will clearly see we're not talking to a man any longer. The passage states:

*vs$^{12}$ Son of man, take up a lamentation upon the king of Tyrus, and say unto him, Thus saith the Lord God; Thou sealest up the sum, full of wisdom, and perfect in beauty. vs$^{13}$ Thou hast been in Eden the garden of God; every precious stone was thy covering, the sardius, topaz, and the diamond, the beryl, the onyx, and the jasper, the sapphire, the emerald, and the carbuncle, and gold: the workmanship of thy tabrets and of thy pipes was prepared in thee in the day that thou wast created. vs$^{14}$ Thou art the anointed cherub that covereth; and I have set thee so: thou wast upon the holy mountain of God; thou hast walked up and down in the midst of the stones of fire. vs$^{15}$ Thou wast perfect in thy ways from the day that thou wast created, till iniquity was found in thee.*

I underlined some important points hinting to who we are truly addressing. Now I don't know about your bible history knowledge friend, but this king was not old enough to have been in the garden of Eden. Also, there was no way that an omniscient God confused this man king with a cherub/angel. God is directly speaking to satan, who was perfect and beautiful to look upon, who sat in the mountain of God until iniquity was found in his heart and he was cast out. Covered in precious jewels to the likes Liberace and Elton John could not rival, and instruments built inside of him because he was responsible for leading the worship in heaven. He was perfect until he was no longer content with being the opening act for God but rather wanted to BE God.

Although the beginning of this chapter was written directly to the prince, he is only the product of a culture that his father entertained. The king's sinful ways made him a perfect puppet of another one who's actions for wanting to be in control and BE God got him kicked out of the presence of God. God dealt with the sin in these men and punish the action. The peculiar part is that God grieved the king because He knew clearly who was really at work, following the strings to the puppeteer, and had Ezekiel document the confrontation for our learning and growth.

Could you imagine if Ezekiel had gotten starstruck or was impressed with the man that was standing in front of him more than the God that he served? What would have happened if he was embarrassed to correct this celebrity family? The demon at work would still have liberty to continue.

We see the same thing in Isaiah chapter 14 where God has Isaiah confront the king of Babylon. Verse 4-11 was for the man; vs12 lets us see God address the real culprit and goes into further detail describing The Sin he committed. As Isaiah describes God's account of what happened, we see satan use the words "I Will" five times. In his heart he had determined to:

- ➢ 1st = Ascend to the highest point in Heaven
- ➢ 2nd = Establish his throne above God's
- ➢ 3rd = Sit in God's Holy Mount
- ➢ 4th = Ascend above the heights of the clouds
- ➢ 5th = Be Like the Most High

The "I" trouble that we see here is an example again of treason on The Highest Throne. In times of monarchy, when treason is committed the punishment is death. The king of Babylon is promised that but also, we see satan receiving the promise of the pit of hell.

The last example is one that is more applicable for our everyday life but a very different scenario. Matthew 16:13-23; (also Mark 8:27-33) Jesus is with the disciples and asks them who do the people say that He is? They offer an assortment of answers referencing some of the great prophets of scripture, then He ask them personally of their thoughts. Peter responded that He was "The Christ, The Son of the Living God". Discerning clearly that God gave him that answer, Jesus speaks a tremendous blessing over him in vs 18 and 19. In vs 21 Jesus begins to tell them of what was to happen at Passover and His dying and being resurrected again on the third day (proof again that they didn't preach the 'gospel' we often refer to today but rather the Kingdom of God).

As an immediate kind of knee jerk response, Peter rebuked Jesus as if to say, "this won't happen to you Lord, I won't let it!" Fresh off his blessing, I guess Peter was motivated out of a desire to protect Jesus, but how does Jesus respond?...

*vs$^{23}$ But he turned, and said unto Peter, <u>Get thee behind me, Satan</u>: thou art an offence unto me: for thou savourest not the things that be of God, but those that be of men.*

Jesus addressed the root of that answer. With the precision of a surgeon He cuts the string that seemed to be motivated out of a good idea in Peter but wasn't a God idea. This last example shows us how anyone can be manipulated if they are not watchful in prayer and being focused on Kingdom culture not even moments after a spiritual high. ANYONE!

As a matter of fact, with the demands of social media and the technology that constantly connects us to the world we slowly lose the time that should have been designated for the Lord. We must get delivered from people. If we allow people to influence us instead of letting the Gospel be our catalyst for how we react to situations, it will begin to cripple us from living our best life. We need discernment to have the ability to be able to see past the people and their actions to identify the source. Following the strings, and by the power of God help them get free (John 8:36).

Now, when I say that, I need you to understand that your fight has to do with the fact that we wrestle not with flesh and blood, but principalities and powers... which is a perfect segway to our next point.

# You Might Be Fighting the Wrong Fight
## Scripture Source (KJV)

Ephesians 6:10-14

Who is our fight with? Well, let's read Ephesians 6:12 : "For we wrestle not against flesh and blood..." Let me stop right there at the first few words of that verse. The reason I want to stop there is because I have to say this differently. If all I say is, 'we wrestle not against flesh and blood' sometimes that seems a little too fluffed. But if I say that people are not your problem, will that help you? I need you to understand that your fight is not with your spouse or the people who live in your house. Your fight is not with your supervisor and it's not with the people who cut you off on the highway while you're driving. Your 'wrestle', your fight is NOT with people. People are NOT your problem.

Pay close attention to this statement: God has not given you power over people.

If He gave you power over people then every time that you gave advice, every time you gave good counsel, every time you told somebody to do something, it would have worked—it would have happened—they would have listened to you—there would have been no issues. And yet, He did NOT give you power over people. God DID, however, according to Luke 10:19:

*vs<sup>19</sup> Give unto you power to tread upon serpents and scorpions, and over all the power of the enemy: and nothing by any means shall hurt you.*

Emphasis given to the underlined portions. You have been properly equipped to face your enemy. In the next verse He even encourages us to not be happy or rejoice over the fact that these spirits are subject to you but rather be happy that your apart of His Kingdom!

Now listen, if you keep fighting people and you keep getting frustrated, the reason is you're fighting the wrong fight.

You can't get frustrated and mad because people do wrong. You must remember that while Jesus was on His way to the Cross, He did not mumble a word. He took a beating that was so bad that He no longer looked like a man according to Isaiah 52:12 and yet He took every lick from the centurions, the crowd, and accusation from the Pharisees, as they escorted Him to Golgotha.

I need you to grab hold of the fact that Jesus did not say a mumbling word. Not because He couldn't or didn't have to but because He was doing it at the request of His Father for these people. He realized that people were not His problem, but rather His assignment.

Maybe, you're fighting the wrong fight.

We waste time, emotion, and effort trying to straighten 'haters.' You don't have any haters. You have ONE enemy. His name is satan. People become tools or allies unknowingly more times than they know in his effort to destroy you.

He hates you because GOD LOVES YOU. That's it.

Now, he realizes that it would probably be too obvious if he was to show up with a pitchfork and a red tail. What's he going to do is get to those people who are behind your wall, behind your line of defense, the people who you love, the people you're connected to or regularly engage with. He's going to try and use them to get into your head and get to you. I need you to understand that they are not your problem; they are not your issue.

People are not your problem. Bad habits are not your problem. Addictions are not your problem. The things that people do or how they operate and respond to what you do, that's not your problem.

What your problem is or who your fight should be with is the enemy.

So, when you talk about who's going to 'catch these hands,' what you need to be doing is letting the enemy catch you praying while you're on your knees, decreeing and declaring "Thus saith the Lord..." so if you have to lift up holy hands demons flee!

---

PERSONAL NOTES: *Now go back and read all the scriptures referenced in this past section and write any New-Gets that the Lord revealed to you since reading this section.*

# 4. The WHAT

## The Enemy Only Steals the Good Stuff
Scripture Source: (KJV)

John 10:10- 12; 1$^{st}$ Samuel 16:1-13; 13:14; Matthew 3:13-17; Matthew 4:1-11; Ephesians 1:10; Psalms 75:6-7

If you happen to inherit a diamond ring and wanted to know how much was worth, would you take it to your doctor? How about your mechanic? No, you would take it to a trained certified gemologist, right? Your mechanic and doctor may be able to tell you that it looks beautiful, or how much they think it's worth but no matter how much schooling or training they have received they are not qualified to properly assess the gem's true value.  The purpose of going to the gemologists is to identify not just it's value but how to properly protect and maybe even ensure the treasure from possibly the only other individual who may be able to properly assess the value:  a master thief.

Jesus declares in John 10:10 that the thief comes to steal, kill, and destroy. No master thief risks his freedom to steal costume jewelry, he wants what you've insured. What the enemy wants to steal from you is your value.

In 1st Samuel 16 David was the youngest of Jesse's sons. Literally, he's the one that no one thought of. When

Samuel the prophet was sent to David's home to find and anoint the new king of Israel, even he had to ask his father if there were any other sons. The Lord confirmed that David was the one chosen by Him and Samuel anointed him as successor to the throne of Israel.

Before that while in the field guarding the sheep, God was preparing and training him. While in the field he learned two things that helped him to realize his value in the eyes of men the way the eyes of God already saw him.

First, David killed a lion and a bear, defending the things that belonged to his father. His desire was to protect the sheep, the flock of the father. He learned how to love what the Father loved.

Second, while protecting the sheep he realized that he was owner of nothing but was responsible for everything that was placed in his care. He mastered stewardship in shepherding that prepared him for the next level in his life. He mastered what he was given and wasn't looking for promotion but rather was setup for it (Psalm 75:6-7).

It had nothing to do with his outer presentation as Samuel was being taught through the process it took for them to get to the chosen one. The Lord literally had to tell him in vs 7 not to make a bad assessment based on the outward appearance. It was an assessment based on the heart matter that only the Lord knew that qualified David. These qualities made him the preferred choice in Jesse's house. What happens when the ones who got picked before you are the ones who get to call you in for your promotion? (as one of my southern preacher buddies would say "man that dog will hunt",...another day)

Later, David is defined as a worshiper whose music God uses to remove a demonic spirit from Saul. In the next chapter he is given a mission where he thought he was delivering a meal, but he ends up 'delivering' a nation from Goliath and God establishes him as a warrior. David, the diamond in the rough, overlooked and despised by men and yet his story, even his writings collected during his time in exile show the value of his heart. To the point that when you read the Psalms you connect with the feelings of brokenness and then remember that there is still hope as you continue through each chapter.

David had a heart so great it was the criteria that God required to serve as the next king in 13:14 once Saul went rogue. God described it as one "after my own heart", and then promised for His Son, Jesus to be born into his blood line when the day came for Him to establish the Kingdom here. What an assessment! What great value. I'm so glad Samuel got a second opinion from God and not trusted Jesse's suggestions.

Let me give you an acronym. It's D.A.V.I.D. The enemy wants to steal your "D.A.V.I.D".
Spelled out it is:


> D = DIRECTION
> A = AUTHORITY
> V = VICTORY
> I = IDENTITY
> D = DESTINY


So, let's break this down into smaller bite size pieces.


## DIRECTION: Follow God's Lead
Matthew 3:15-17; 4:1; Psalms 37:23

In Matthew 3:15-17, Jesus is baptized by John the Baptist who remarked that he felt unworthy to touch the laces of Jesus' sandals. Jesus told him, "Suffer it to be so..." Let it happen.


And a voice (Father God) spoke out of Heaven: "This is my beloved Son in whom I am well pleased." Then the Holy Spirit in the form of a dove descended on Jesus head. The power of the Holy Spirit rested upon Him. Immediately afterwards, He was led by the Holy Spirit into the desert to fast and pray and be tempted, .


The first thing the enemy wants is to steal your direction. Jesus had just come out of the water. He just got open confirmation of who He was based on The

Father's words spoken over Him from the cloud. In other words, He operated His identity based on the Father's assessment of Him, not what people spoke over Him. He got, His assignment, His purpose, His power and His direction, with emphasis on being led by the Holy Spirit.

The enemy wants to steal your direction. Distraction is the first step on the road to Destruction. If all the enemy can do is divert you from God's designated path just a little bit... Like a car that is misaligned, after a while it's going to start wearing on your tires; then it's going to start wearing on other mechanical components in the car. It's trying to go a different way because you have not corrected its alignment. If left in this state, unintentionally, you begin to drift over the lines of your lane into dangerous oncoming traffic. If you're going too fast or fail to pay attention and you overcorrect you destroy the vehicle and possibly end your life.....before you reach your destination!

The moment that Jesus was in alignment with the purpose of what the Father had spoken over Him, He got direction. Before there was Garmin, or GPS trackers, long before phones got smart, we had maps. I remember my father planning our summer route from New York to Georgia every summer as we would break out the map and determine the path. If we didn't have the map we wouldn't know where to go.

What does the enemy want to steal from you first? DIRECTION. One degree of diversion totally changes your destination.

## AUTHORITY: Behold I give you
Romans 4:17; Proverbs 18:21; Isaiah 55:11; Luke 10:19
Job 22:28-29

The next thing that the enemy wants to steal from you is your AUTHORITY. How do I know this? What happened when the Holy Spirit descended upon Jesus? He got Power, right? He wants to steal your authority. I already referenced this earlier. If God used words to frame the universe and then fashioned us to be like Him, then we should believe the fact that we have the power of positive confession into existence just as He did (Romans 4:17).

Remember if God gave you power over all the power of the enemy, the only way the enemy is going to get power is from you. So, every time that we say, "This car never works when I need it", "Oh, I hate this job" or "This place is just the devil" –well, guess what? It will be the devil (like hell) for you. Why? It's because we 'spoke' it. In Proverbs 18:21 it reads,

*vs²¹ death and life are in the power of the tongue: and they that love it shall eat the fruit thereof.*

Notice how the scripture quotes "Death" first, we defaultly begin our conversations in a pessimistic manor. Our comments if not intentionally reviewed before being spoken sabotage our victory as well as the lives of others.  Man, if we could only see the words that came out of our mouths as we spoke them, we would change our idol unintentional conversation. Isaiah 55: 11 states:

*vs[11] So shall <u>my word</u> be that <u>goeth forth out of my mouth</u>: <u>it shall not return unto me void</u>, but <u>it shall accomplish that which I please</u>, and <u>it shall prosper</u> in the thing whereto I sent it.*

 If we spoke our words like the Father, expecting them to do something, then we would realize that they were like ammunition in this battle we are in. Prayers like missiles, decrees like automatic weapons, blessings like bombs we would be making effective warfare. Unfortunately, most of us complain more than we confess. The moment that we say those things, the enemy is like "Ooh, another bullet...Ooh, another a grenade she dropped... I can't wait until he...says something else. Keep the pressure on him and he will complain some more"

Ever heard someone shout, "Why are these kids always acting up?!"  Listen to what has been spoken over the children—remember they are just seeds and our words have power—what happens ten years from now when the words spoken over them begin to manifest. "You never listen..." Guess what, now they're incarcerated because they don't listen. Job 22:28-28 coaches us on how to empower people with the power of our words. It reads:

*vs²⁸ Thou shalt also decree a thing, and it shall be established unto thee: and the light shall shine upon thy ways.*

*vs²⁹ When men are cast down, then thou shalt say, There is lifting up; and he shall save the humble person.*

Eliphaz encourages Job as he is going through his tribulation telling him to use his words to change his situation.

In Genesis 3 we see the devil operate as a serpent but in Revelations 20 he is described as a dragon. So, my question to you is, who fed the serpent? We did! Generations of conversation where we whine instead of win and worry instead of worship. Surrendering valuable ammunition and power to a usurper. Remember, your authority is powerful, and the enemy wants to steal your authority. If he can steal your direction and authority, he gets the opportunity to get momentum.

## VICTORY: You are part of a winning team
Genesis 2:7; Matthew 6:33; Psalms 24:8; 1ˢᵗ Peter 2:9-10; Romans 8:37; John 15:15

Next letter is V. With the Kingdom of God comes VICTORY. You got victory the moment that you allowed Christ to become King over your life. Ephesians 1:10 describes how it is the desire of the Father to unify all things in Heaven and Earth together unto His dear Son, Christ Jesus.

It's not just the desire of the Father that Jesus be the King of Heaven but also King of the Earth. The earth is us. (Genesis 2:7) He gave the earth to Man to have dominion over it so if He is to save and change the world it has to happen in the hearts of men. Men who then submitted to His Kingdom culture, change the world to meet His standard of living also known as His righteousness (Matthew 6:33).

There's a reason why all through the Scripture He's called King of Kings. He needs you to relinquish your 'crown', your will, and your ways to Him.  Like a conquering king who rides through territories that each have their own laws, currency, and languages. When they are taken, they become part of a greater unified kingdom. The benefit is that they no longer are responsible for the weightier matters of independence only compliance. They lose their laws, customs, ways, language, and even currency because they are under watch care of the King. Their enemies are now His enemies, their problems become His. In every man's heart there's a Cross and there's a Throne. You can only be on one. You can only choose one. You can't half cheek the Throne with God and expect results. Once submitted to even touch the throne let alone sit in it is treason.

When choosing the throne for where you're going to serve, to be in control and make your own decisions, you immediately crucify Christ afresh.

And yet, if you surrender your 'crown' and let him be King of your life, you allow Him to reign on the throne of your heart. The moment He becomes your King, Psalms 24:8 describes Him as "...the King of Glory. The Lord strong and mighty, the Lord mighty in battle". We're talking about a King who has never lost a battle—an authority that has no rival. The moment we allow Him to be King over us, we immediately become partakers of victory, a chosen generation, a royal priest hood, and a peculiar people (1st Peter 2:9-10). Jesus even describes us at that point as more than conquerors (Romans 8:37), and friends (John 15:15).

## IDENTITY: Remember who you are

Matthew 4:11; 3:15-17; Revelations 12:10; Jeremiah 1:5; Deuteronomy 28:13, Isaiah 26:3; Mark 9:29; John 14:9

The next letter is I, for IDENTITY. In Matthew 4, you will see specifically where the tempter comes, and he immediately begins his onslaught with "IF" you are "the Son of God". Now, just like John the Baptist and everybody else who was there when Jesus came out of the water, they all heard God specifically say, "This IS my beloved Son in whom I am well pleased."

Who witnessed this happening? Yes, John the Baptist and the Apostles but also, satan.

Now, if satan can question Jesus, know that he will do the same about your identity. Revelations 12:10 describes him as the "accuser of the brethren" which means to me he is going to accuse you of things you did do, and even some things you didn't do just to try to get you to question God's assessment of you. You know, trying to knock down your value because of a few bumps, scrapes, and bruises we've collected along the way.  Asking if you're really called to be in ministry, if God really loves you, are you worthy to be used after all you did last summer... you get the idea. Whether He has called you to pastor your office of co-workers, or evangelize your school, we've all been called.

Sometimes people confuse an office or title with a calling. You can operate in the calling and not have the office or title. Unfortunately, sometimes when people can't find their identity in God, they look for it in a title. Since they can't find their contentment in God alone, now they've got to find their contentment, their peace in an office or a title and not in their calling. These are the type whose insecurities are only quelled when you call them by their title or office before you call their name, or they are constantly in pursuit of the next level to distinguish their place in the body of Christ. I'm just waiting for new ones like Pas-sionary (Pastor/Missionary), or like my high school buddy John would say, Proph-ostle (Prophet/Apostle), or Rev-angelist (Reverend/Evangelist).

I'm defined by what I walk in because God spoke it over me. There is a prophetic and apostolic grace on my life, but you won't catch my Facebook changed to that. When I stand before the Lord at judgment, ..... hopefully He'll call me 'Vincent' – prayerfully He'll call me by the name He has for me written in a stone (Revelations 2:17) – and hopefully I'll make it. Believe me, there are a lot of people who preach on this side of the pulpit to that side of the church, who aren't going to make it. I pray that I do. In the event that I do, I'd love for Him to call me Vincent. I would be cool with that. But if He wants to call me Hammerhead the Third, honey I'll be Hammerhead the Third.... and praise Him forever saying "Holy, Holy, Holy!" love HH3.

Pay attention. It's not the office. When you understand where your identity comes from, when the Lord spoke over Jesus and called Him– Son -that was enough.

Peace comes to a restless heart when we understand that our identity is based on what the Lord speaks over us. Not our experiences, not what we came out of, not what people call us, not our failures, our issues, our hang-ups, or our old habits.

You are what God speaks over you.

Your identity is based on what He called you from before you were formed in your mother's womb (Jeremiah 1:5). If the enemy can steal what God spoke over you, make you forget and forfeit what God still speaks over you, you can get caught up by him trying to take you to a place of unforgiveness.

Finding yourself fighting to feel worthy and accepted by a God who is not surprised by anything you do or have done. Why, because He already knew about it before you did it and before you were called.

If the enemy can make you forget that you've been called to be "the head and not the tail," (Deuteronomy 28:13) and you don't focus on the One who can give you "perfect peace"(Isaiah 26:3) – then the enemy can rob you of perfect peace because you don't know who you really are.

In Matthew, Satan challenges Jesus's identity: "IF you are the Son of God..." What did he say? "...command these stones to become bread." Now, he's not even dealing with the victory that Jesus had over a 40-day fast and how most of us cannot make it through one day of fasting without accidently putting something in our mouths. [That's a whole other message for another time].

Mark 9:29, Jesus tells us that fasting, and prayer need to be a regular part of our lives in order for us to get victory in some areas. When we grab hold of the process of what it takes for us to operate in sanctification and not just being saved but set aside for His use, being compliant to His righteousness or standard, THEN our identity is based on what He speaks over us.

The more I do what the Bible states and act the way He requires of me, guess who I'll begin to look like? Like HIM.

The more I do it, the less they see of me and the more they see of HIM. Jesus said, if you have seen Me, you've seen the Father. (John 14:9) Paul encourages the Colossae church in that the world may see the treasure of our identity being, Christ in us the Hope of Glory. (Colossians 1:27)

My identity is based on reflecting His purpose, His mission, His call. To summarize I will borrow a line from a powerful story of a king to his son who allowed the lies of the enemy to run him off from his kingdom, position, and post, and cause him to forget what was spoken over him as a boy. Mufasa says to Simba in the Lion King, "Remember"

## DESTINY: Your testimony of God in the earth

2nd Samuel 7, 12; 1st Chronicles 28, 29; Deuteronomy 6; Hosea 4:6; Proverbs 22:6; Luke 15:11-32

The last letter stands for DESTINY, better known as your legacy or ministry.

What really was David's true specific purpose? He was anointed to be king, but 2nd Samuel 7 describes a beautiful friendship between God and David. The Lord loved him so much that He pretty much said, "Listen,

I'm going to make sure that I send my Son in your bloodline."

In other words when you operate in your D.A.V.I.D, it makes it so that generations that follow you can walk in victory that previously they could not have because you did your part. Solomon could not have built the Temple if David had not prepared and assembled the materials during his tenure (1st Chronicles 28, 29). He laid a foundation of relationship with the Lord in the good times and the bad. When he was good, and when he was being corrected for his actions because he owned up and truly repented. Like for example with Bathsheba in 2nd Samuel 12 when confronted by the prophet Nathan.

The greatest thing you can leave for your people to inherit is not land or cash. If they aren't wise in their dealings those will be lost. An inheritance of the power of relationship with our King is the greatest. If satan can keep us from fulfilling the responsibility of cross generational sharing about who God is and who they are to God to the next generations, our enemy benefits greatly from their ignorance. (Hosea 4:6)

Let me explain... The power of a cross generational testimony of who our God is requires at least three generations to participate. The first is the Patriarch / Matriarch generation. Then the Children/ Parental generation and lastly the Grandchildren / Seed generation.

➤ The Patriarch's responsibility is to frame a good foundation and their message is to show through faithfulness, consistently over time we find that "God is Able".

➤ The Parental Generation is similar in responsibility only their message is "Don't do my stupid". They are not old enough to be an example of God being consistent through the ages but can clearly show God can deliver.

➤ The Seed Generation benefits from getting a tried and proven framework lived in front of them that is confirmed by two generations. Their job is to grow into the examples of what has been deposited in them by example so when they graduate to the next level the process continues.

This is what I feel God meant when He said teach our children and our children's children in Deuteronomy 6.

The enemy wants to steal your 'D.A.V.I.D..' So, what is it specifically that he wants to steal? Your Direction, Authority, Victory, Identity, and your Destiny.

If you get off course, guess who's following you? If you don't model a prayer life in your home, guess what your children will never have?

Have you ever seen someone try to force their kids to model a culture and get mad when their kids don't respond? Out in a public place and tell their kids to pray and the kids are like, "What, we're going to pray for real?" Embarrassed, now the parent pushes the issue "Come on, Pastor said pray over the food. Stop acting like you don't know how to pray." It's unfortunate but it doesn't have to happen.

We are urged to train up a child in the way he should go (Proverbs 22:6), it didn't even say it had to be your child. Sometimes you may be the voice that another kid will hear and prayerfully someone else will serve as confirmation to your kids in the day that your voice seems too distant for them to hear.

That is why the prodigal son's Father was able to stand looking down the street every day, with hope and anticipation. He knew that what was deposited would come to fruition at some point. (Luke 15:11-32)

---

PERSONAL NOTES: Now go back and read all the scriptures referenced in this past section and write any New-Gets that the Lord revealed to you since reading this section.

# 5. The WHERE

## Establish the Home Court Advantage
### Scripture Source (KJV)

Joshua 24:15; Matthew 6:24; Ephesians 6:11; Romans 12:1-2; Psalms 51:5; Philippians 4:7-11

We should be working hard not to forget that we are in warfare all the time. We have an adversary. There are two specific warring kingdoms—the Kingdom of God and the kingdom of darkness. And, whether we choose to believe it or not, we are either an ally or in full-fledge allegiance to one kingdom or the other. This is why Joshua says to Israel, "choose ye this day whom you will serve" and then makes a bold declarative statement about his family choosing to serve the Lord (Joshua 24:15). In Matthew 6:24 Jesus says:

*vs²⁴ No man can serve two masters: for either he will hate the one, and love the other; or else he will hold to the one, and despise the other. Ye cannot serve God and mammon.*

It is impossible to stand on the top of two mountains at the same time, and you cannot be a double agent in this war. The idea is we want to be able to win our battles. To win this fight, it's not going to happen by saying, 'God will win my battles' or by singing songs or worshipping. This requires a daily intentional choice. We must understand and apply proper battle tactics daily so that we can successfully win.

It doesn't mean that we always get it right. What it means is that the more we practice the tactics, the more proficient we become. The more we effectively apply them, then the more success we will have in our lives. Now before you say you've read this already, remember, repetition breeds retention, so I may review certain points in order to hammer home a concept.

In a previous chapter, I specifically taught about WHO the enemy is. Oftentimes, we fight the wrong fight because we end up fighting who we think it is—people but Ephesians 6 specifically tells us that we battle not against flesh and blood. In other words, ...say it with me:

"People are not our problem"

We must get delivered from people. People are not our issue. So, stop getting upset with your ministry team, your co-workers, or your friends. The enemy loves to use people who are close to you, who are behind your defenses. The enemy won't ever try to come at you or try to intimidate you with a pitchfork and a red tail because that is too obvious; but if he used your kid to get right on your nerve or used your spouse... Now watch this. It's not so much that it's your spouse or your children or your boss. It's the spirit operating or trying to use them to cause you to lose focus and to forget that there's an eternal fight going on so you will take it personal. When you take it personally, you lose your power! Luke 10:19 states the Lord has given us all power over the enemy.

The power of the enemy is spiritual. That's why when you tell people to do stuff and they don't do it, it's because God didn't give you power over people. He gave you power over all the power of the enemy.

So, speak to demons. Speak to generational curses. Speak to the assignment of the enemy. Cancel those! You can't cancel people.

We also identified the What the enemy wants to take from us, but now we'll learn about Where the battle is currently taking place. More times than not, we think the WHERE is at the job or on your local traffic route when they drive erratically. You know, like spiritual wickedness in low places. Let's look at some other mistaken venues, like someone tries to take over your living room TV and keeps hiding the remote. Or, someone is taking forever in the bathroom. The truth is that your home, office, school, or car is not where the fight really happens. This is where you experience the physical manifestation of the enemy forces trying to advance on you, but this is not where the fight is happening. The real battlefield is the Mind. Let's get some scripture in here to help support the point.

Beginning at Romans 12 :1-2:

*vs[1] I beseech you therefore, brethren, by the mercies of God, that ye present your bodies a living sacrifice, holy, acceptable unto God, which is your reasonable service. vs[2] And be not conformed to this world: but be ye transformed by the renewing of your mind, that ye may prove what is that good, and acceptable, and perfect, will of God.*

Revisiting the idea that we were born in sin and shaped in iniquity (Psalms 51:5) Paul is telling the Roman church that we defaultly have hosted a home court for the enemy in our minds. He challenges us to change the standards and have our mind "transformed" from the world's standards and way of living to the standards of righteousness found in the Kingdom of God.

Have you ever been to a pro or college sports game and noticed the end zones and court floors have been painted? You could tell who the host team is based on the colors, emblems, and logos strategically placed all over the arena. Why? It's because it's their arena, their house. You have come into their house. They have the 'home court advantage.' In other words, the fans that have filled the stadium should be cheering for the one to whom that stadium belongs to. Each one, expressive in their own way, from body paint, to jerseys, costumes, and headdresses. They come to represent and support the home team.

Rungrado 1st of May Stadium, better known as the May Day Stadium, located in Pyongyang, North Korea is the largest stadium in the world. With a height of 197' it seats 114,000 fans, including the breezeways and the field a staggering 150,000 total capacity. That is humongous!

Imagine that your mind is twice the size and you are personally responsible for filling the stands and security. That seems almost impossible to reason and yet the Lord already has a plan set for that. Like any good team/ arena owner, He knows how to fill and secure it. Remember when I said your problems become your Kings problems when you are submitted to and focused on Christ?

Isaiah declares, He will keep you in perfect peace when your mind is stayed on Him (Isaiah 26:3). That same peace of God, which is beyond our reasoning, or like I like to say "makes no sense", because when others are frantic you operate in a level of peace that is literally out of this world. To solve our stadium security issue, what you do is let the peace of God oversee security because Paul says it will guard our hearts and minds through Christ. Read Philippians 4:7-9:

*vs[7] And the <u>peace of God</u>, which passeth all understanding, <u>shall keep your hearts and minds</u> through Christ Jesus.*

*vs[8] Finally, brethren, <u>whatsoever things are true</u>, whatsoever things are <u>honest</u>, whatsoever things are <u>just</u>, whatsoever things are <u>pure</u>, whatsoever things are <u>lovely</u>, whatsoever things are of <u>good report</u>; <u>if there be any virtue</u>, and if there be <u>any praise</u>, <u>think on these things</u>.*

*vs[9] Those <u>things, which ye have both learned</u>, and <u>received, and heard</u>, <u>and seen in me</u>, <u>do</u>: <u>and the God of peace shall be with you</u>.*

## Grow the Fan Base, Sell the tickets

Now we need to fill the stands of the stadium of your mind, with the fans that celebrate your God. How do we accomplish this? Well, Paul is encouraging us as he did the Philippian church to have a season ticket holder sale for "Things". Things that are True, Honest, Just, Pure, Lovely, Good, Virtuous, and Encouraging. Things that they have learned since becoming Kingdom fans. Testimonies of His greatness, memories of His mercy, Songs of deliverance. Things that they have received via impartation and teaching, and things they have seen modeled in front of them by their teachers. As a result of them filling the stands with these "Things" Paul says the God of Peace will be with them.

When you invite those things into your mind it changes the atmosphere and your attitude. Now it's impossible to shut out fans of the other team. Somehow, they always get tickets too but we have to fight thinking of all the things that have gone wrong, all the missed opportunities, all the people who did us wrong and we kept score. All that does is give the enemy some fans to make noise on his behalf. All that stinking thinking is just scalping tickets to unsavory fans of failure. For an example of the power of the fan:

September 21st, 2019 the University of Georgia hosted a rematch against Notre Dame at Sanford stadium with an attendance of almost 94,000 fans including an additional 500 seats that were promised for Notre Dame fans just for this game alone. Georgia fans are notorious for their participation and sports reporters credited the fans as the number one contributing factor to the Bulldogs winning that game. The noise level was so loud that the Fighting Irish missed plays, creating errors due to their inability to properly hear their strategies in such an aggressive atmosphere. When I think of filling the stands of our minds this is the picture I have. That the season ticket holders in my mind rejoice over what God is doing in my life so loudly, that it foils the plans of the enemy.


Keep your mind focused on God. This is where you get the home court advantage. So, when your enemy comes on the field to try to get victory, you can turn the results because he has entered in a place that is filled with the memories and the fans of the fact that "God can", "God will" and "He's not done yet". You get to boldly tell him:

"Yes, I've might have messed up last season but not today satan, it's my winning season! If you try to accuse me about my past, Revelations tells me about your future! My future is destined in the fact that my King reigns and I'VE GOT THE HOME COURT ADVANTAGE!"

Be confident friends because if God be for us, who can stand against us!

---

PERSONAL NOTES: *Now go back and read all the scriptures referenced in this past section and write any New-Gets that the Lord revealed to you since reading this section.*

# 6. The WHEN

## Your Enemy Is Not Making Appointments
Scripture Source (KJV)

Matthew 6:10; Luke 18:1

We must be reminded that we are always in constant warfare. There's the kingdom of darkness and the Kingdom of Light. There is a King who reigns over all things, which is Jesus Christ. According to Ephesians 1, it is the Lord's will and His desire to unify all things in Heaven and in Earth together unto His dear son that He can reign over all things. So, when we pray the prayer and we say, Lord, let your kingdom come and let your will be done in Earth as it is in Heaven (Matthew 6:10) we are answering that prayer.

We also have to remember the fact that as sure as there is our King, there is also an adversary that goes around like a roaring lion seeking whom he may devour (1Peter 5:8).

There is a clear enemy and we learned about WHO he is. We also learned WHAT he wants to steal, your D.A.V.I.D.. We've determined WHERE the battle is going to happen, your mind.

Now, I'll tell you WHEN to expect him. Unlike the bully in elementary who threatens to black your eye after school, your enemy is not going to make an appointment.

Listen, He's not going to ask you when he can show up to whip your tail. He's not going to tell you when he's going to steal your joy, create strife in your marriage, or mess with your children. Neither will he RSVP to impose generational curses on the people who are coming after you. The enemy doesn't make appointments, which means he doesn't work by our standard of Time. Let me illustrate...

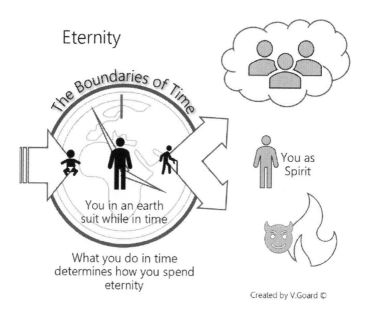

Eternity

The Boundaries of Time

You in an earth suit while in time

You as Spirit

What you do in time determines how you spend eternity

Created by V.Goard ©

In the graphic, I have pictured us as we go through the life cycle. We are spirit beings that have an eternal soul and operate in an earthly suit. Just like when an astronaut travels to space and puts on a space suit, well on earth, our flesh is our earth suit. When we are born, we put on flesh and it is subject to time. It is what we do in our earth suit while in time that determines our eternal destination. Whether in Heaven with our Lord or in Hell with the enemy. This is why when Jesus came to earth, He told God prepare me a body (Hebrews 10:5).

I need you to grab hold of the fact that we first serve a God who lives in Eternity. Unfortunately, so does our enemy, he is not confined to the walls of time like us. In truth, our adversary is not constrained by it but rather benefits from it. As a spirit being, he can wait you out. He'll try and see what he can get to work on you because he has had the time to do a case study on your family.

With time working in his favor, he remembers what was successful with your grandparents and other family before them. He wants to try and see what he can pull on you because he's outside of Time. Do you see now the importance of cross generational deposits of the testimonies of God in the family? If we don't know that someone dealt with a similar situation but was delivered or that the Lord made a way for a previous generation, the current is doomed to fail for the lack of information.

Having said that, understand that there are some "times" where eternity and the battlefield, our mind, intersect. That's WHEN he likes to fight.

There is an acronym used for addiction recovery patients that fits so well for our WHEN. The acronym is H.A.L.T. The definition of the word halt is to stop or cause a process to be ended. Doesn't that sound like a tactic of our enemy? Spelled out the acronym is:

- ➢ H - HUNGRY.
- ➢ A - ANGRY
- ➢ L – LONELY
- ➢ T – TIRED

So, let's look at how the enemy would like to end your process.

## HUNGRY: What are you broadcasting

The first letter is H-Hungry. Seeing as we have been commanded by our King to include fasting as part of our regular routine, we can condition the flesh to ignore hunger pains but that's not the hunger I'm talking about. I'm talking about the thing that drives you on the inside. You know, it's that unspoken desire that we allow to be broadcasted by our actions or subliminal speech. Just like a war codebreaker the enemy picks up the 'signal' and tries to meet that desire, that hunger.

For example, when you feel like you are not getting the kind of attention that you need or you feel that you're underappreciated, you feel that 'hunger.' Guess what the enemy will do, send agent #42 to give you the attention that you want... but from the wrong person, the wrong way.

Remember now, people are not the problem, and most times they don't even know they are being used. If you fall to the hunger, you are being used also in the same moment. The people that the enemy may try to trick into using are not the issue. He understands that the 'when' for you is when you're hungry.

This is the first one but probably the most dangerous because this hunger can manifest in different ways and can become the stumbling block for many leaders. The desire to be respected among your peers can place individuals in a steeplechase for degrees that only rack up loans and fill a wall full of plaques but leaves the heart empty. Even in the natural, you will compromise your standards when you are hungry.

# ANGRY: Don't miss the Promised Land

Next is A, for Angry. Ephesians 4:26-7 states:

*vs$^{26}$ Be ye angry, and sin not: let not the sun go down upon your wrath:*

*vs$^{27}$ Neither give place to the devil.*

In other words, anger will happen over time. What you do with the time when you're angry makes the difference. This one is a perfect example of how what we call a feeling is in actuality, a WHEN that bridges time and eternity.

Remember when God was angry with Isreal and Moses talked Him down from striking them off the planet? Exodus 32:12-23 is an amazing chapter that begins with God being angry with Isreal and Moses reminds Him that the world saw how He delivered these people in powerful demonstration. Surely the world will mock if it seems that God only delivered them to slay them in the wilderness. Now, I don't believe that Moses' argument was what changed God's mind. We are talking about the one who knows the end before the beginning. I enjoy the idea that even though He was already resolved in His heart what He was going to do, God still vented to His trusted servant. It was in this conversation that God was able to hear the heart of Moses to gauge his response also.

Moses and Joshua walk down from Mount Sinai with the tables of God's Law to hear what Joshua thought was war in the camp. Only the more seasoned ears of Moses would clarify, saying the sound they heard was singing. As they get closer, Israel is engaged in full on idol worship and the one left in charge only had excuses. Can you just hear Aaron, like "Moses, man, you know how these people always playin' ...they were like 'Moses been gone too long', 'make us a god' and then brought me a bunch of gold from Egypt and.... then out popped this golden calf. For real Moses, honest!" Here is the powerful part, the very one petitioning God for Him to stay His anger, lashes out in anger casting down the tablets and causing a chain reaction. He burns up the idol, mixes it with water and makes them drink it.

It would be this same Anger that later the people would stir in Moses due to complaining that would cause him to miss the promised land (Numbers 20:11)

The enemy loves for your anger to show up. When your anger shows up, you lose rationality and you operate outside of the guidelines of spiritual standards. In other words, you are no longer operating in righteousness. You're no longer seeking God's kingdom and His culture. You're looking for revenge. You're keeping score. That's not how our King operates. God says forgive, not to keep score. He promises that vengeance is His in Revelations 12:19 and that He will repay for the aught lobbied against you.

Remember, when you are subject to the King, your issues and problems become His. Here is the why reason Jesus tells us to pray for our enemies and for those that use us (Matthew 5:44).

## LONELY: You are not alone

Lonely is next. Lonely is not just when you're by yourself in your house or when you're the only one in the car when driving. Lonely is a mindset. Remember now, if the mind is the battlefield and lonely is a mindset then that becomes a WHEN for the enemy to attack. You can be in the middle of a crowd, interacting with people, and still feel lonely. Yet it is also possible to be alone in a room and feel the presence of God and know you are not alone. It's the enemy's desire for you to feel that the Lord is far and not omnipresent. When you pray, you must make it past the stars just to be heard.

Friend, Hebrews 13:5 promises us that He will never leave you or forsake you. When we don't spend time meditating on His promises and growing in understanding, we slowly loose our sense of His presence. Like water evaporating in a glass, there must be a continual replenishing which is why Jesus promised the baptism of the Holy Spirit to be our comfort, teacher, and guide. Therefore, the enemy would love for you to feel those lonely moments, so he can capitalize on your feelings and attack.

## TIRED: Keep Pressing!

The last letter is T-Tired. I can't tell you the number of times when failure happens when exhaustion sets in your mind—the battlefield. Compromise presents itself as an option when you feel like yawning, "Aagh, next time" or "You know, I just need some Me-time" when instead you should be on your knees. It's at that moment when your standard starts to waver. Knowing how frail our natural bodies are, the Lord established fail safes for us. Watch how the Lord promises to be our strength in time of fatigue. Isaiah 40:28-31:

vs$^{28}$ Hast thou not known? hast thou not heard, that the everlasting God, the Lord, the Creator of the ends of the earth, fainteth not, neither is weary? there is no searching of his understanding.

vs$^{29}$ He giveth power to the faint; and to them that have no might he increaseth strength.

vs$^{30}$ Even the youths shall faint and be weary, and the young men shall utterly fall:

vs[31] But they that <u>wait upon the Lord shall renew their strength;</u> they shall mount up with wings as eagles; they shall <u>run, and not be weary</u>; and they shall <u>walk, and not faint</u>.

God pretty much says, "I don't get tired, and those who serve Me won't either". We would never get to experience the supernatural if our natural was enough. It requires us to get to a place where we absolutely must trust that the circumstances set before us God has already prepared for so when we don't feel like we are enough, He gets to be more than enough for us. Friend, this journey is not a sprint but rather a marathon. Don't rush God's process, be patient and press through. (LUKE 18:1)

H.A.L.T. is the WHEN the enemy will advance.

_____

PERSONAL NOTES: Now go back and read all the scriptures referenced in this past section and write any New-Gets that the Lord revealed to you since reading this section.

# 7. The WHY

## You Get His Old Room!
Scripture Source (KJV)

Isaiah 14:12-14, John 3:16, Jeremiah 29:11 Ephesians 2

Why would the Enemy want to fight you so?

Now remember, we have a specific enemy. It is satan. It's not people. In Isaiah 14:12-14, you'll see where he specifically describes satan getting kicked out of Heaven. Remember, we identified that satan is our problem. He's who we have our fight with.

Can you recall the day you moved out of your family home for whatever reason? While you're gone, your room was changed, and you come back to visit only to find out that your parents don't have space for you anymore. Your room has been changed to an office, a home gym, a library, a music room, or whatever. The space that you thought was yours got changed. Well, it's kind of like that. Almost. The difference is satan was the one that was removed, and God is now preparing for us to sit in heavenly places with Him in Christ Jesus. (Ephesians 2:6; Revelations 19:1-19; 21:1-6)

Let me be clear, God doesn't love the sin but is willing to walk you through repentance to save you from you (John 3:16). In fact, one of people's favorite verses to quote is Jeremiah 29:11. It talks about "the thoughts I [God] have for you...good and not evil...to bring you to an expected end." Really, that's God talking to His people, the Israelites when they're in bondage after they've done wrong. Pretty much what's He's saying is even though you've done wrong, I still have great plans for you. I love you. You're not what you did. I have great things in store for you...even though you must sit through this correction.

The reason that you're involved in this whole big battle in the first place is because the Lord absolutely loves you. You look like Him. Read back in Genesis . You're made in the image of God. So, every time satan looks at one of us, He's got to be reminded of the One he stood up against in Heaven.

God loves you. He absolutely loves you. He loves you in spite of all you've done, despite who you think you are, what you've come out of, or even where you've been. He loves YOU. Your adversary however is trying to get you to do the same thing he did to get kicked out so you can share in his eternal punishment. To choose your own way, sit and exalt yourself to the position of king of your own life and sit in the rightful place of God.

Now let me say this to you. The enemy hates the idea that you look like God and that God has given you creative authority over the Earth—the very thing he was kicked out of Heaven to be on. And then, when God started working and formed the Earth, He gives dominion on Earth to MAN. This means satan has been displaced from Heaven and he has no jurisdiction here on Earth!

Hell is where satan is to be committed to for eternity. At some point, he's going to be chained. He's going to stand for judgment. Read Revelation. There's a point when he's going to be released but again, the idea is that satan has an end. He's already sentenced and currently out on bond. He already has an ending. For someone who doesn't have any future of value, he's mad at the fact that you've got his old room. That you have been invited to participate in the marriage supper with Christ Jesus. You get to be invited to the New Jerusalem and to see the Throne of God. You get to be invited with the 24 elders to join in the eternal worship service, "Holy, holy, holy!" for Eternity.

Why does the enemy hate you? One reason. God loves you. HE LOVES YOU. He loves your dysfunctional, funky, still trying to make your way through-making bad decisions but trying to make better ones Self....

Yeah, all that. God loves you and that's why the enemy hates you so much. That's why you're part of the battle.

---

PERSONAL NOTES: *Now go back and read all the scriptures referenced in this past section and write any New-Gets that the Lord revealed to you since reading this section.*

# 8. The HOW

## You're Not Prey. Look Out For T.R.A.P.S.!
Scripture Source (KJV)

1 Corinthians 10:13; James 1:13

Just to recap.

Our fight is with satan. People are not our problem. God didn't give you power over people. He gave you all the power over all the power of the enemy. People are not who we're fighting with. Where we're fighting is not in 'flesh and blood'—not in this realm or this reality. The actual battlefield is our mind. When we fill the stands in the arena of our mind with things that "...are lovely, that are just, and are of good report" we allow the memory of the things that God can do to be season ticket holders, we establish a home court advantage for the Kingdom of God. As always, the enemy tries to sneak a thought in there that doesn't belong, but if we are intentional, I promise you there will be more fans in the stands cheering for the King of Kings so you can have a winning mentality. What he wants to steal is your Direction, Authority, Victory, Identity and he absolutely wants to steal your Destiny.

Now, we'll learn HOW the enemy will fight you. Paul declares it is imperative that we know this or satan could gain an advantage over us (2 Corinthians 2:11). We cannot choose to be willfully ignorant of his devices. The importance is so you won't be blindsided by how he's maneuvering. I've got another acronym. It's the word T.R.A.P.S.. Now the word is defined by itself already. It lets you know that it is a tactic in which to try to enslave or entrap a victim or a prey. Spelled out it is:

➢ T = TEMPTATION
➢ R = REBELLION
➢ A = ATTITUDE
➢ P = PEER PRESSURE
➢ S = SIN

Remember, 1 Peter 5:8 declares that the enemy goes about as a roaring lion seeking whom he may devour. He's acting like a predator because he wants you to think that you are prey. If you adopt the mindset that you're prey, you won't pray but rather surrender authority and lose your momentum. That's how he sets his T.R.A.P.S. in motion.

## TEMPTATION: Don't take the bait
James 1:2-4; 1:12-15; 1 Corinthians 10:13

First letter of the acronym is T-Temptation.

For years our Men's ministry at our church have gone on fishing outings to bond and fellowship. When we go out, I promise you, I look the part. Tackle and poles in a monogramed travel bag, lures, even live bait. Unfortunately to this day, I could be standing right next to a man pulling fish in and all I get are sticks. For whatever reason my bait was not interesting enough no matter how far or deep I cast. We even rented a boat once ...to no avail for me however for the other brothers, they do their research and land the big catches. I shared that to say this. If the enemy knows what your weakness is and what your preferences are, one of the first things he's going to do is 'go fishing' with bait specific to what he his trying to catch. What does a fisherman put on the hook? Bait...your Bait!

He's not going to tempt you with bait that you aren't interested in. For example, my wife is a sports head, and an avid football fan. She enjoys Rom-Coms, action, and hero movies. So of course, watching these movies with her I discovered what her "type" was. Her favorite leading man is tall, dashing good looks, dark skinned, with .5% body fat. Sort of like a Morris Chestnut, Idris Elba, with a side of Dwayne Johnson, Vin Diesel, and a dash of Chris Helmsworth to round the formula off. If you have ever seen me, um well.... I'm a little closer to baby Groot than "the Rock". I used to get offended, but my father taught me to relax because I get to take her home after we go see her eye-candy at the theater.

Now, knowing her type, there was no way the enemy could bait her with a Danny DeVito style temptation.

James 1:2-4 is an amazing chapter on temptation and it begins with him telling us to be excited when we are tempted. Can you imagine that, he elaborates provoking us to find joy because the trying of our faith triggers patience, which grows us into spiritual maturity. Here is the important part:

*vs[12] Blessed is the man that endureth temptation: for when he is tried, he shall receive the crown of life, which the Lord hath promised to them that love him.*

*vs[13] Let no man say when he is tempted, I am tempted of God: for God cannot be tempted with evil, neither tempteth he any man:*

*vs[14] But every man is tempted, when he is drawn away of his own lust, and enticed.*

*vs[15] Then when lust hath conceived, it bringeth forth sin: and sin, when it is finished, bringeth forth death.*

Vs 12 tells us that there is a reward called the Crown of Life that comes with overcoming temptation. 13 defines that this is an enemy exclusive tool because God doesn't use this in His arsenal.

Vs 14-15 show that each bait is custom made and activate The Sin protocol which if not remedied with repentance result in death, both natural and spiritual. The enemy knows exactly what you're susceptible to.

The power of bait is that it is normally hidden in plain sight, made to look like it is natural or supposed to be there. 1 Corinthians 10:13 states:

*vs[13] There hath no temptation taken you but such as is common to man: but God is faithful, who will not suffer you to be tempted above that ye are able; but will with the temptation also make a way to escape, that ye may be able to bear it.*

Temptation shows up in other forms also and are not as obvious but are just as dangerous, even habit forming and deadly to the point you cannot get free of them. For example, demonic cues or witchcraft hidden in children's television and movies to make the occult common and the demonic familiar. Now your house is infiltrated with the items that belong to a different kingdom. Why target the kids, because they are the most trusting. Here is why it is important to operate with spiritual discernment as we are responsible to teach our families to identify and resist the devil that he may flee (James 4:7)

The bait is temptation. You can beat it but if you chase or take the bait, it's the difference between winning and losing. You may, like the fish, nibble and dabble with the bait...you may even get away with it once or twice. But one day the fish that is persistently curious gets eaten.

## REBELLION: It don't really take all that, does it
1st Samuel 15:23

Next letter is R-Rebellion. Rebellion!? It stands for those times when you question whether the level of intensity for the integrity of the righteousness of God is necessary or not. The scripture states in 1st Samuel 15:22-23:

*22 And Samuel said, Hath the Lord as great delight in burnt offerings and sacrifices, as in obeying the voice of the Lord? Behold, to obey is better than sacrifice, and to hearken than the fat of rams.*

*23 For rebellion is as the sin of witchcraft, and stubbornness is as iniquity and idolatry. Because thou hast rejected the word of the Lord, he hath also rejected thee from being king..*

What I want you to think about is that rebellion is not the big things like apostasy (abandonment of religious belief). It's the small stuff like, "Oh you know, I can drink because I can hold my liquor!" or "I'm just a sinner saved by grace". If you are choosing to operate in righteousness, then it means that at some point in your walk with the Lord you'll choose not to do certain things—just because you don't want His standard to be compromised with your witness—because you want to show the world who God is. It doesn't mean that you'll get it perfect every time, but it does mean that you choose to do something different. It also does not mean that this relationship is a bunch of do's and don't's, that's religion. Relationship drives me to love Him like He requires and not how I desire.

People always find scripture to try and justify their small sins like, "You know Jesus turned water into wine. That was His first miracle!" but that is the portion that I am referring to. If you are a new convert, a babe in Christ, I can understand you having some habits and ways that are still common to you. As you grow to know the Lord better and get discipled somethings you should just choose not to do any longer because the word of God convicts you to maturity. I choose not to drink not because what were to happen if the person I am fellowshipping with has a real problem with alcohol. It's not to shame them to abstain, it is to not be the reason that they stumble deeper in a whole because His righteousness requires it.

## ATTITUDE: You can control it
Philippians 2:5

A-Attitude. How you go into and react to a situation lets you know if you're going to be victorious or not.

Philippians 2:5 simply declares,

*Let this mind be in you, which was also in Christ Jesus*

Let me summarize this point, I don't want to minimize this but this one requires self-discipline. For a season in the early 2000's we had this whole 'What Would Jesus Do' movement permeating the Body of Christ. Better known as W.W.J.D., it was a great way to curb a very sensitive issue as attitudes are often connected to feelings. Paul encourages us to not trust our feelings but rather fight the feeling to model the behavior and character of Christ.

So, when you go to the local Walmart and there are 32 registers but only 6 are open and there are no self-checkout lanes, and the shortest line is already into the women's clothing section... Control your Attitude! Maybe the line was long so you could pray for someone in it.

When the customer service is below par at your favorite restaurant and when you ask for the manager only to realize that the person who was serving you was the manager-on-duty.... Control your Attitude! You have no idea what they endured today, and the Lord specifically let them be the ones to serve you. Not for you to give back what you got but so you in turn could serve them by asking about their life, pray, encourage, and leaving a tip regardless of the poor service they knew you experienced. My wife and I often get opportunities like this only to have the server break down in tears or even chase us out to the parking lot asking if we really meant it. It's not to get glory, but FOR His glory. I cannot tell you how many God inspired moments we as believers miss when we have the wrong attitude. God knows what you can handle, You got this.

## PEER PRESSURE: Well, everyone else is doing it
Psalms 1:1-12; Proverbs 13:20; Romans 12:1-2;

You'll be surprised how often we make the mistake of being subject to other people's desires. It's amazing how social media makes us a slave to peer pressure—looking for a certain amount of 'likes'—looking for a certain amount of endorsements as if they could actually add value to us. Unfortunately, instead of pleasing an audience of one, the Lord, we often find ourselves trying to please a group of people—to move the masses of people to be garnered to our side rather than the alternate. Yet, if we lose them to gain Him, then we truly win. David begins the Psalms with this:

*Psalm 1:1-3*

*vs[1] Blessed is the man that walketh not in the counsel of the ungodly, nor standeth in the way of sinners, nor sitteth in the seat of the scornful.*

*vs[2] But his delight is in the law of the Lord; and in his law doth he meditates day and night.*

*vs[3] And he shall be like a tree planted by the rivers of water, that bringeth forth his fruit in his season; his leaf also shall not wither; and whatsoever he doeth shall prosper.*

It's in the choice to follow the instruction of God's Kingdom Culture that the one who chooses to turn from herd mentality finds prosperity and favor. Association breeds assimilation, whatever you hang around is what you will begin to mirror so be careful to not let bad company corrupt your good character (1st Corinthians 15:33)

## SIN: The Separator
John 1:29; Genesis 3; Isaiah 14:14-17; John 8:34; Matthew 4:17

The last one is S for Sin. I want to be specific about THE Sin. First let's reference John 1:29:

*vs²⁹ The next day John seeth Jesus coming unto him, and saith, Behold the Lamb of God, which taketh away <u>the sin</u> of the world.*

John the Baptist sees Jesus and knows what His divine purpose is, declaring from afar that He came to remove "the Sin" from the world. Notice again he doesn't reference Jesus coming to die on the cross or resurrection. It is to address the treason the world is committing by choosing their own way, being absent from the Kingdom of God.

If we use the principle of first reference to define it, the first time we see the sin, in the eternal timeline, Lucifer commits it in heaven as recounted in Isaiah 14. Ejected from Heaven we see him next on earth when talks men into committing sin in Genesis.

Unfortunately, it would only multiply and grow with each generation of men. Like a seed sewn, what starts off as disobedience to God's command in Adam and Eve, multiplies into jealousy and murder in their son Cain against his brother Able. Later we read the sin grow so rampant that in chapter six through nine we see God wiping the earth with the flood and beginning again with Noah and his family. Every action of sin, Helping the kingdom of darkness grow as we become slaves to The Sin (John 8:34 YLT).

The Sin is you choosing your will over God's. In the book 'The Gospel Isn't (Just) About Me', Palmer &

Alexander call it, "The first sin --- which is the root of all sins --- is the desire to be the King, the one who sits on the throne, THE Sin".

It's the day that you choose to take authority instead of letting the Lord be King over your life. It is manifested in many ways. For example, when I steal, who does it benefit? Me. When I lie, who am I covering? Me. When I cheat who receives the pleasure? Me. Do you see the pattern?

| The Sin culture says: | Kingdom culture says: |
| --- | --- |
| Do as thou wilt | Not my will but thy will be done |
| You only live once | I'm living to live again |
| Everything in moderation | Only if my Father does it |
| Just follow your heart, it will guide you | Love the Lord with all thy Heart, Soul, Mind, and Strength |

When you choose Sin culture, it keeps you from allowing Christ to be on the Throne of your heart. In every man's heart, there's only one Throne and there's only one Cross. You can only be on one of them. In truth we are being saved from ourselves, but also being saved TO something, the Kingdom of God. If it were not true Jesus' first words on assignment would not have been to announce it in Matthew 4:17, *vs[17] From that time Jesus began to preach, and to say, Repent: for the kingdom of heaven is at hand.*

Heralding a warning that a decision must be made, and a price paid because judgement requires the treason to be dealt with. If you choose to be on the throne then you crucify Christ, again. But if you choose to be on the cross, then you mortify your flesh or deny it of it's selfish, sinful, urges to let Him be King of your life, you have a better chance of not falling into 'traps.' Remember, your enemy is trying to get you to do what he did to get the punishment he got.

_____

PERSONAL NOTES: *Now go back and read all the scriptures referenced in this past section and write any New-Gets that the Lord revealed to you since reading this section.*

# 9. Expanded Breakdown

## The Enemy's Forces
Ephesians 6:12

In these chapters, we established that people are not our problem. We have established: Who our enemy is, What are his targets, When, and Where he'll attack you, Why he does it and How.

In Ephesians 6, Paul sticks this one verse in the middle of the armor of God analogy. There are plenty of books, studies and lessons on the armor of God but not many that expound upon the verse I am referring to. The Lord shared something as we were going through Battle Tactics that I feel is necessary for you to hear.

It is specifically about the enemy's support forces. As described in Ephesians 6:12, it states:

*vs¹² For we wrestle not against flesh and blood but against principalities, against powers, against the rulers of the darkness of this world, against spiritual wickedness in high places*

It breaks down in one short verse the forces of the enemy and it identifies them. The best way that I can probably describe these forces is comparing them to our own nation's armed forces: The Army, the Marines, the Navy/Coast Guard and the Air Force. Well in this war the enemy has branches too, and he fights us on two separate fronts.

The first front is the physical with what I want to call the ground forces. This is based on the fact Genesis 2 states we were created from the "dust of the earth" and so the enemy wants to fight you in your flesh, in your body, in the 'dust.' Hence the term ground forces. The other front is the spiritual attacks that the enemy puts together. These two together, both the physical and spiritual make for a powerful assault.

## GROUND FORCES: Army & Marines

Let's look at the first two, 'principalities and powers.' Principalities are often described as areas where demonic influence is strong. For example, a sin that is predominant in a region or area would be called a principality. Certain things that are synonymous in cities or certain regions by which they are known. But for you as an individual, principalities reference the list of principles (beliefs or standards) that you live by.

You know people who have principles that supersede God's law in their lives. You'll watch people do things and justify it with "it's the principle of the thing." They'll fight in areas where they shouldn't be, instead of letting God's standard be the higher standard. Here's where the principalities put them in a situation where they're fighting in the 'flesh.' The best way to describe that is like the Army. The enemy's army specifically does this: it brings guidelines or rules that makes it so that we live by a certain standard and keeps us from living by God's standard. Just like the Army, they are more powerful in plural, meaning the more you have the stronger the principalities have authority in your life.

The second one referenced in the verse is Powers. I want to liken that to what would be our Marines. When you send the Marines, you don't send a lot of them. They are all specialized, they are tenacious, and they are trained at a different level than the Army is. When we talk about powers of the enemy's ground forces, when he fights our flesh, these powers operate like addictions, habits, and generational curses, Things that specifically attack the flesh but operate on a stronger level than just what a bunch of life rules could (principles). We're talking about an enemy that has taken the time to study you and your family. Remember, we fight against an enemy that lives outside of Time. Time does not box him in. Having said that, he's had the opportunity to watch what worked on your grandmother, what worked on your auntie, what worked on your uncle, what worked on your great - great – great grandfather.... You get the idea.

Those things which end up looking like generational curses are just the enemy using time to his advantage- -to use certain things to try to attack your flesh or your ground forces. These are the kind that require the fasting and prayer Jesus described to get deliverance from.

## SPIRITUAL FORCES: Naval & Air Forces

The spiritual parallel to the Navy/Coast Guard in the enemy's arsenal is subtlety described in Ephesians 6:12 as "the rulers of the darkness of this world". I need you to remember that when you're forgiven of sin, Micah 7:19 specifically states that the Lord takes your sin and throws it into the "sea of forgetfulness." Pay attention. In the natural the Navy is free to sail open seas but when certain waters are established you need permission to enter them. The enemy does not have the authority or the power to affect you, to overcome you, to beat you. So, he's going to try to get you to give him authority.

Here's where his navy comes in to attack you in the spirit realm.

Yes, you're forgiven but what his navy wants to do is cross borders to take you into the "sea of forgetfulness". The idea is to make you fish out things that only you have the authority to access. God forgave you and He threw your sin into the "sea of forgetfulness" for a reason. Even God is not interested in them returning. He is not interested in wasting precious time dwelling on forgiven things when he has a plan for your life.

The enemy doesn't have the power to pull it out, so he tries to use accusatory tactics to make you fish out things about who you used to be. So, he'll say "You know what you used to do" or "You know where you've been" or "You know where you came from." When you begin to dredge those things out, it cancels or negates your forgiveness. Drowning you in the despair that you will never be totally accepted by God when that is not true. That is the purpose of the enemy's naval fleet.

The other military power I want to share with you is the enemy's air force or the "spiritual wickedness in high places." So how is the enemy's air force described? If you look at Daniel 10:12, you'll specifically read how Daniel prayed a prayer. When the angel from Heaven came in response to his petition, he told him as I paraphrase, "Listen, from the first day you started praying God heard you and sent me with the answer. But, for 21 days the enemy (the prince of Persia) blocked or buffeted me from coming to the point that Michael the Archangel had to come and help me!"

Now, why do I call "spiritual wickedness in high places" the enemy's air force? The purpose of this attack is to frustrate your prayer life. Can you imagine if Daniel had stopped praying? Even though God heard him the first day and sent the answer. What if you got your prayers answered immediately after you prayed? Tell the truth, we would not pray as much.

Here's why "spiritual wickedness in high places" wants to frustrate your prayer life. If the enemy can keep you from being persistent and being faithful in prayer over the course of time, however long it takes, until you see what needs to happens

My former pastor and grandfather, Johnnie Corbett, used to say, "Kneeology never hurt no body son. Pray until something happens"

Continue until you see the promise manifest. If you give up before your answer comes, you won't get the opportunity to see the enemy's air force defeated.

I need you to understand through that one verse, that just as sure as we have natural armed forces that collaborate to defend the nation, our enemy also has forces.

Here's the great thing about this fact.... Don't forget that the Lord has given you power over all of that. No matter what his ground armed forces do when they come to fight you. When the spiritual attacks come to try and make you fish in the "sea of forgetfulness" or frustrate your prayer life, don't stop—don't give up.

Your assistance comes when your faithfulness continues to press through. It is not over. You're not finished. God has an assignment for you and when you allow God to be your "General" and to fight for you. You Win.

## A Blessing

Friend, I pray the Spirit of the Lord bring back to your mind all that you have learned in these pages. So that as you go forward you will clearly begin to see the spiritual mine field that the enemy would love you to fall into. I decree the grace of God empower you to be point for others to as they navigate their way through their trials to our King. May the Anointing of God compel you to preach this Gospel that heals broken hearts and frees captives. Praying your discernment be sharpened as you attain the prize of the high calling in Christ Jesus, amen.

# References

Palmer, D., & Alexander, C. (2016). The Gospel Isn't (Just) about Me: Surrendering My Kingdom to Him.

# Suggested Readings

Compass by Toemeika Goard

Divine Design for Discipleship: Following God's Blueprint for Spiritual Development by Chad M. Craig

Daily Wisdom from the Who: Impartation from the Gospel to Transform Lives by Buckmire/ Bradford/ Clark/ Goard/ Holmes/ Jones

# Contact

 @VGoard

#SeeChristInEverything
#5MinFridays
www.VincentGoard.com
www.FaithDeliveranceTemple.org

Made in the USA
Lexington, KY
13 November 2019